MANAGING YOUR DEBT

Intelligent Options for Gaining Control
From Canada's Leading Debt Relief Specialists

JOHN & JENNIFER CROFT

This book is dedicated to all of our brave clients who let us walk alongside them during their financial crisis and be a positive influence in their lives. It has been a privilege and a pleasure to serve you. We are forever grateful for your friendship and support.

We want to thank God for giving us the opportunity to learn valuable lessons about how to use money as a tool to help others. We thank Him for giving us the ability to help people in our community. We are grateful for our team of gifted employees, who are just as committed to helping those in need as we are.

Finally, a special thanks to Craig Ware, who has been an incredible friend. Thank you for helping us communicate what was in our hearts and minds with excellence and clarity!

The information contained in this book is intended solely to provide general guidance on matters of interest for the personal use of the reader, who accepts full responsibility for its use. The information is provided with the understanding that the authors and publishers are not providing or intending to provide legal, accounting, tax, or other professional advice or services. As such, the information contained in this book should not be used as a substitute for consultation. Further, we are not Licensed Insolvency Trustees and do not offer the services of a Trustee.

While the authors have made every attempt to ensure the information contained in this book has been obtained from reliable sources, the authors are not responsible for any errors or omissions, or for the results obtained from the use of this information. All information in this book is provided "as is," with no guarantee of completeness, accuracy, timeliness or of the results obtained from the use of this information, and without warranty of any kind, express or implied, including, but not limited to warranties of performance, merchantability and fitness for a particular purpose. Nothing contained in the book shall to any extent substitute for the independent investigations and the sound technical and business judgment of the reader. Laws and regulations are continually changing, and can be interpreted only in light of particular factual situations. Getting professional advice before taking any action for your particular circumstances based on the information contained in this book is strongly recommended.

CONTENTS

INTRODUCTION

We Know What You're Thinking . . .

DOES THE WORLD REALLY need another book on how to get out of debt?

Big banks, popular authors, and reality TV shows bombard us all the time with advice on how to be debt-free. There are pop-up ads, magazine ads, radio ads, and it seems like every monthly magazine devotes space to how to deal with crushing debt.

While these ads can be great resources, most of them will offer you the same advice. Some "experts" will suggest you pay off low-interest debt first, while others encourage you to pay off the high-interest debt first, but most advise you to consolidate all of your debt at a lower interest rate in order to have one monthly payment.

That is sound advice, but what about the people who have already tried budgeting programs yet are still struggling to make a dent in their debt? What happens when you follow all of the "expert" advice and still cannot save for your family's needs?

If you have already tried cutting expenses but simply cannot reduce your debt no matter what you do, this book is for you. It's not going to provide you with a quick-fix solution to your debt problems. (Guess what? Those do not exist.) Instead, this book will educate you on all the different debt relief options out there. We hope one of them may make sense for you.

Ask yourself this: If you could pay off your debts within the next 10 years (at full interest) but come out of it with no savings, no investments, and nothing to your name, would you still be ahead? What if we told you there is a better way to get rid of your debt and increase your cash flow, sooner rather than later?

This book will give you all the answers.

We have helped thousands of Canadians reduce their debt in the communities we serve. We've worked with a lot of people who are struggling financially. We know it is not an easy journey to navigate and can often feel like a lonely road. Don't despair. We will make sure you have a clear understanding of all of your options so you can make the best decision for you and your family.

We know firsthand what happens when a person is overwhelmed by debt. The negative impact of debt extends far beyond just the monthly minimum debt repayments. It impacts your quality of work, rest, and sleep. It affects your ability to be the parent, husband, or wife you want to be.

Most debt solution books are written by Americans. Not ours. You can learn a lot from American authors, but ours is written "by Canadians, for Canadians," because we have different regulations when it comes to debts, loans, mortgage lending, bankruptcies, and consumer proposals.

Are you ready to change your life for the better? Let's get to work.

The examples and testimonials provided in this book are from real clients. Their names have been changed to protect their identities.

In the first section, we will cover debt repayment options that will not affect your credit rating. The last half of the book will deal with options that will affect your credit rating but may be better in the long run, depending on your circumstances.

CHAPTER 1

Meet Dick and Jane

MEET DICK AND JANE.

They have been married for almost 10 years and have two young children, with another child on the way. Dick runs his own handyman company, while Jane works part time in the local bookstore. Together they bring in about $5,000 a month after taxes. With their mortgage, car payments, and other household bills, they are struggling to make ends meet.

They had access to a lot of credit but lacked the proper knowledge, skills, and discipline to manage their funds responsibly. Their financial illiteracy caught up with them and it's impacting more than just their pockets. They fight as a couple and admit they are in over their heads. The stress of money is affecting their marriage as well as their relationship with their kids, extended family, and friends.

They own a nice home, which they bought several years ago when real estate prices were high. They were told if they didn't purchase right away they would miss out on some great real estate opportunities.

Dick and Jane are maintaining payments on two leased vehicles and have never been late on their payments. Dick has three credit cards and Jane has two. They have a joint unsecured line of credit and a joint overdraft on their chequing account. When you combine all of their credit cards, lines of credit, and overdrafts, they have unsecured debt totaling $63,684.

This means they are paying approximately $1,600 a month just to keep up with the minimum payments on these products.

They are desperate to make things right and find a suitable solution to repay their debts. Having been referred to us by a friend, they started a written correspondence with us.

CHAPTER 2

Consolidation Loans

DEAR JOHN AND JENNIFER,

We hope you had a chance to read the financial brief we sent you.

As you can see, we are both working full-time with a decent monthly combined income of about $5,000. We are never late on our minimum monthly credit card payments, but we can't seem to reduce our debt.

We have a variety of credit cards, a little bit of overdrafts, and an unsecured line of credit as well as a mortgage and a car payment.

We feel trapped in this vicious cycle of debt, so our friend Jacob recommended we contact you. Our debt is causing a strain in our marriage and affecting the quality of our family life and friendships.

Can you please help?

Sincerely,
Dick and Jane

DEAR DICK AND JANE,

Thank you so much for writing us. We know what it's like to struggle with debt. You feel overwhelmed and frustrated, and it's hard to see any way out. The good news is we can help.

Having reviewed your financial statements, we can immediately point out why you are struggling to make headway on your debt. Simply put, it's the power of compounding interest working against you.

Compounding interest is paying interest not only on principal but also the previous interest already accrued. Unfortunately, that allows your debt to grow exponentially, and eventually it becomes extremely difficult to catch up.

You should be aware some credit cards charge compound interest on a daily basis. For example, let's say you have a revolving balance of $10,000 on your credit card, with a daily interest rate of 0.041% (which is approximately equivalent to an APR of 15%).

Multiplying $10,000 by 0.00041, you'd pay an interest of $4.10 on the first day. On the second day, the interest would be charged on a new balance of $10,004.10, which means there will be a new principal amount due every day and it will keep compounding daily until it is paid off. So you are not just paying down the original principal balance, you are also paying down the interest accrued on that balance each month.

We highly recommend you read the fine print on your credit card statement so you know exactly how your credit card interest is calculated.

For your particular case, it looks like all of your credit cards are maxed out. You have interest rates ranging between 11.99% and 23.99%. That means, thanks to the compound interest, it will take years before you can pay it off.

I went to an online interest calculator site called www.calculatorweb.com to give you an idea of the kind of compounding interest you are dealing with. Based on the information you provided us, your credit card interest alone (excluding your overdraft and line of credit), based on your current minimum payment of $1,346/month, would total $30,345 with a payment schedule ranging from 33 months to 136 months.

This is what I saw; I apologize in advance for adding salt to your open wound.

REPAYMENT TIME

How long will it take to completely pay off my credit card bill?

Calculate how many months it will take to pay off your credit card balance and the amount of interest you will pay during that time, based upon the interest rate that you enter.

Credit Card Balance:	$ 13684
Interest Rate (APR):	17.99 %
Payment Amount Per Month:	$ 411

Calculate

Months to pay off debt:	47
Total interest you will pay:	$5414.10
Total to pay back:	$19098.1

REPAYMENT TIME

How long will it take to completely pay off my credit card bill?

Calculate how many months it will take to pay off your credit card balance and the amount of interest you will pay during that time, based upon the interest rate that you enter.

Credit Card Balance:	$	11736
Interest Rate (APR):		11.99 %
Payment Amount Per Month:	$	235

Calculate

Months to pay off debt:	70
Total interest you will pay:	$4600.36
Total to pay back:	$16336.36

REPAYMENT TIME

How long will it take to completely pay off my credit card bill?

Calculate how many months it will take to pay off your credit card balance and the amount of interest you will pay during that time, based upon the interest rate that you enter.

Credit Card Balance:	$	8840
Interest Rate (APR):		21.99 %
Payment Amount Per Month:	$	177

Calculate

Months to pay off debt:	136
Total interest you will pay:	$15212.59
Total to pay back:	$24052.59

REPAYMENT TIME

How long will it take to completely pay off my credit card bill?

Calculate how many months it will take to pay off your credit card balance and the amount of interest you will pay during that time, based upon the interest rate that you enter.

Credit Card Balance:	$	2644
Interest Rate (APR):		14.99 %
Payment Amount Per Month:	$	53
		Calculate

Months to pay off debt:	79
Total interest you will pay:	$1522.71
Total to pay back:	$4166.71

REPAYMENT TIME

How long will it take to completely pay off my credit card bill?

Calculate how many months it will take to pay off your credit card balance and the amount of interest you will pay during that time, based upon the interest rate that you enter.

Credit Card Balance:	$	11780
Interest Rate (APR):		19.99 %
Payment Amount Per Month:	$	470
		Calculate

Months to pay off debt:	33
Total interest you will pay:	$3596.14
Total to pay back:	$15376.14

REALITY CHECK

WHAT ARE YOUR OPTIONS?

The most common step is to consolidate all your debt into one monthly payment.

We recommend you talk with your bank or financial institution about obtaining a loan large enough to cover all your debts. This would allow you to combine your debts into one payment while preserving your credit score. One monthly payment will also better fit your budget, since it has a lower interest rate and can hopefully be paid off in the next five years.

There are some "watch-outs" you need to know. For example, most banks will only refinance their own debt, so if you have a line of credit with one bank and a different credit card with another bank, they will generally only offer you a consolidation loan on the debt you owe them. This has everything to do with risk.

Bank A will not take over a debt from Bank B because they'd be responsible for both debts. Whenever a bank lends, it lends with a "what if something goes wrong" philosophy. Banks want to limit risk, so they will secure your debt to something you own (like a house or car), or they will simply turn you down to avoid the risk altogether.

It is often a more difficult process to get a consolidation loan in these situations, but let's assume you do get approved. Here's what you should look for.

First, what is the true cost of the loan? It's a really easy formula:

TRUE COST = PRINCIPAL × Interest Rate × Length of Loan

Let's say the bank approves you for a $64,000.00 consolidation loan at 8%. The payment will be $1493.33 a month over the course of 60 months. Doing the math: 64,000.00 × 0.08 × 60 = $25,600.

So this loan of $64,000 is going to cost you $89,600.00 (in total) to pay off. Before you sign, you need to be aware you will be paying $25,600.00 in interest over the next five years.

We're not saying to refuse the loan; we just want you to understand the true cost of it. Some banks will say you can always pay off the loan early if you have the funds. Unfortunately, most people do not pay off their loans early, especially if money is tight.

You should know that your bank may try to "securitize your unsecured debts to your assets," like vehicles, investments, and even personal property. This means that if you apply for a consolidation loan, your bank may assess your personal property and hold it as collateral against your loan. Your bank may also ask you for a cosigner or guarantor to protect the interest of the bank.

We want you to be aware that if you are unable to make your monthly payments, the bank can seize your secured assets. Then you would still be in debt and also lose your vehicle or home.

Being parents of young children, you should ask yourself: is it worth the risk?

We don't want you to think consolidation loans are all bad. They lower your monthly payments, give you a little more cash flow each month, and keep your credit score intact. And in some cases, you can obtain one without giving up security (or getting a cosigner) if your credit score is still decent. If you decide to take this route, it would be a very good idea to temporarily set your credit cards aside (such as in a safe) and contact your creditors to reduce your credit limit as a safeguard to prevent you from racking up more credit card debt in the future.

We suggest that you keep exploring your options, doing your homework, and reaching out to us for help.

Respectfully,
John and Jennifer

CHAPTER 3

So You Need a Cosigner

DEAR JOHN AND JENNIFER,

We took your advice and went to our bank for a consolidation loan. Unfortunately, because of our financial situation, they require a cosigner. Jane's grandma said she would be glad to cosign, which is good news.

We are sure that once we get the loan we can get back on our feet. Should we re-apply for the loan?

Sincerely,
Dick and Jane

DEAR DICK AND JANE,

Good question. There are several things to consider before reapplying for the loan. We know you are thinking, "If we could just get that money, everything would fall into place." But unfortunately, it is rarely that straightforward.

The bank has offered you a ray of hope with the option of a cosigner. Take a minute to think about why the bank asked for a cosigner in the first place. They are professional money managers, so they have a clearer picture of your debt than you may want to admit. Now consider the financial risk you are asking Jane's grandma to take on as your cosigner.

When someone cosigns with you, it is NOT a 50/50 split on the debt. You are both now responsible for 100% of it. If either of you fails to pay, Jane's grandmother will owe 100% of your debt.

If it's okay, we'd like to share a story that you may find helpful.

Spending $50 When You Only Make $40

The year was 2008 and the real estate market in Calgary was at its peak. "Rhonda" was a client who made good money. She was a registered nurse, working two jobs and making over $40 per hour, plus overtime. Even though she and her husband "Bill" made great money together, when they wanted to buy a home, the bank required a cosigner.

Why? Because they were high risk in the eyes of the lender.

Although Rhonda made $40 per hour, she spent $50 per hour. Bill and Rhonda's solution was to ask Bill's sister and her husband to cosign for the mortgage, which they did.

Bill and Rhonda bought their dream home. Stores were offering great incentives, so they bought a living room and bedroom set with no interest or payments for six months.

They noticed that their vehicle no longer matched their new lifestyle so they replaced the older (still fully reliable) vehicle with a brand new SUV. Now everything looked perfect. They were finally happy.

Things started to come apart two years later. Bill's sister and her husband were preparing for their retirement, unaware of the impending financial storm coming their way. Bill and Rhonda's mortgage company called them asking for mortgage payments because they had not made a payment for the last two months. The relationship between the two families began to strain.

Bill and Rhonda came to our office looking for help. We sat down with them and went over their vehicle loan contract. They had been paying 29.99% in interest! They were shocked. So were we.

Bill and Rhonda never looked at the true cost of upgrading their vehicle; they were too distracted by the excitement of driving something shiny and new.

Bill and Rhonda lost their home to foreclosure, their new vehicle to repossession, and were left with only one choice: to file a bankruptcy. We wish the story ended here, but it didn't.

The Collateral Damage

The nightmare was passed on to Bill's sister and her husband in 2010. Since Bill and Rhonda purchased the home at the peak of the market, then lost it at its very lowest, when the home was finally sold, they took a $150,000 loss.

Who was going to pay the loan? The Canadian Mortgage and Housing Corporation, who insured the lender as it was a high ratio mortgage, sued the sister and her husband. Why? Bill and Rhonda had already filed a bankruptcy, so CMHC could no longer pursue them for the debt.

Fortunately, we were able to help the sister and her husband settle the debt for a lot less than $150,000, but that isn't the point of the story. The lesson is, when you ask someone to cosign for a debt, they must be prepared to take over all the payments in the event you fail to pay.

That is a big responsibility.

Before Jane's grandma agrees to be your cosigner, you need to have an honest conversation with her about the risks involved. Seriously think about whether it is worth it. If you want our advice, when in doubt, just say no to cosigners and cosigning.

It's not worth the risk of losing relationships with loved ones because of financial conflict that could arise.

Respectfully,
John and Jennifer

CHAPTER 4

Honey, I Found an ATM in Our Home!

DEAR JOHN AND JENNIFER,

Thank you for knocking some sense into us. What can we say? We love our grandma. While taking your cosigner advice may save our relationship with her, it doesn't solve our debt problems.

What about using our home equity for the loan? Is that a good idea?

Sincerely,
Dick and Jane

DEAR DICK AND JANE,

Yup, grandmas are pretty special, eh? As for using the equity of your home, there are a few things to consider.

First off, people who get home equity lines of credit (HELOCs) are generally able to consolidate their debt into one lower monthly payment. When you apply to refinance your home, the hope is always to obtain the best interest rate on that second mortgage.

To qualify for a best rate, the mortgage lenders look at the following qualifications:

1. **LTV, or in simple English, Loan to Value.**
   This is the ratio of what your home is worth divided by how much you owe against it. For example, let's say your home is worth $400,000 and you still owe $200,000 on your mortgage. If you divide $400,000 by $200,000, the loan to value percentage would be 50%. The higher the percentage, the less equity there is on your home; the lower the percentage, the more funds they can securitize from your home. So, yes, it is harder to use your home as an ATM to get a loan. Once a loan is over 80% of the value of the home, it can be challenging to obtain a second mortgage.

2. **Credit score.** You generally need at least a 650 beacon score for a best-rate loan. Higher is always better. Some banks look at 680 as an ideal score, but

even if you have a score of 620, it is possible to get a best-rate mortgage. The lenders will also be looking to see if you have had any collections, judgments, or late payments in the past two years. Any negative marks will reduce not only your credit score but also your chances of getting a best-rate mortgage.

3. **TDS (Total Debt Service).** Determines how much of your gross income is going toward your debts, including your home expenses.

If you pass these three main criteria, you will likely qualify for a best-rate second mortgage. Now the question is what kind of mortgage should you apply for? A variable rate mortgage, a fixed rate mortgage, or a home equity line of credit? There's no "one size fits all." They all have benefits and downsides.

If you want stability, a fixed rate mortgage is best. If you want to save some money by betting that the prime interest rate won't increase too much, then a variable rate mortgage is a great option.

Home equity lines of credit can be a really useful tool for someone who is good at budgeting and saving. But if you are looking to consolidate all your debts into a home loan, this isn't your best option.

HELOCs only require "interest-only payments" and don't require you to pay back any principal of your outstanding balance. This may trick people into thinking they have cash flow, because the payments are very low, but if they don't use the additional funds to make more than interest-only payments, then they will never pay off their mortgage.

With a regular mortgage, you are paying both interest and principal.

What smart people do to pay off their HELOC faster is ensure that all sources of income are paid into their HELOC. They only withdraw the funds they need out of the line of credit, which hopefully leaves some savings in the HELOC, which can help pay down the HELOC faster. This takes discipline and (often) professional guidance and assistance.

A second mortgage is a good option if you want to save your credit score from getting damaged. You should have more cash flow due to the lower new monthly mortgage payments. Instead of paying off your credit cards at 11% to 23.99%, now you only have a monthly payment based on a lower interest rate.

Based on your current debt, we would estimate you only need to pay $400 a month. That's a big drop from $1,260.

If you do get a second mortgage, be wary of the interest rate. It can be as low as your bank's best rate or as high as 30% from a private lender when you calculate the interest, lender fee, broker fee, and potential documentation fee. The payments can vary from interest only to a combination of interest and principal payments.

Before you run off and get that loan, we want to offer you a word of caution. We have met a lot of people who use their home equity to pay off their bad debts. But if you talk to them two years later, guess what? They end up owing the same amount of money all over again.

How could this happen? Simple: their spending habits didn't change. People get in the habit of using their homes like an ATM and without good financial management practices can't curb their own spending habits.

Make a sustainable and realistic budget for you and your family today. The hard part comes after you have done that: you have to live within the healthy boundaries you've set. No cheating!

Credit cards should NOT be used for emergencies. High-interest credit cards are not going to help you buy your way out of debt. That's what emergency savings are for. Finally, we always recommend that you have at least six months' worth of savings that can easily be accessed should there be an emergency or unexpected expenses. Good luck!

Respectfully,
John and Jennifer

CHAPTER 5

Subprime Mortgages

DEAR JOHN AND JENNIFER,

We took your advice and spoke with a broker. He told us that even though our credit is "good" we still have too much debt for our income and not nearly enough equity in our home to consolidate all of our debts.

Apparently the big banks won't lend to us either. The broker said we would need to shop a secondary market for the mortgage. Is that a good idea?

What does "secondary market" even mean? It sounds like another name for "subprime."

Sincerely,
Dick and Jane

DEAR DICK AND JANE,

We are sorry that it didn't work out. The response you received from your mortgage broker is actually pretty common.

Unfortunately, your hunch is correct about secondary markets. They are just another name for subprime. In 2015, some lenders changed the name from subprime to "nonprime" to try to get away from its notorious reputation.

Subprime mortgages are risky affairs. They're the same as bank loans, with an interest rate generally between 8% and 16%, depending on market conditions. Why the higher interest rate? People's home values usually don't rise as quickly as their debts. Which means your debt will quickly outstrip your home's ability to pay for it.

This is why you are considered a higher loan risk (creditwise).

With all that said, we still believe that shopping a secondary market is a decent option if there is already some equity in your home, but be warned: it still may not be enough to consolidate all your debt.

As you have experienced when your mortgage broker tried to get a second mortgage from prime lenders, you still "lacked the equity," which means getting you that second loan would be challenging and costly.

Fees, Fees, and More Fees!

When we say "costly," we mean there are usually at least two to three different bank or lender fees involved, all of which can vary in cost.

The most common fee is the lender fee. Generally, the larger the loan, the larger the fee, and even if the loan is small, say $15,000, it could still be as high as $3,000.

The second-most common fee is the broker fee. This is how your mortgage broker gets paid. This generally is very close to the lender fee amount but can sometimes be as low as $1,500.

The third, less common fee is a documentation fee. This is sometimes known as the application fee, and it's usually between $500 to $1,000.

There are also legal fees. You have to pay a lawyer for your side of the mortgage, which is generally around $800. Sometimes the lender will charge you for their lawyer fees as well. It may seem unfair, but that is the way they do business.

The final fee is the appraisal fee. This is an upfront fee and generally the first fee you pay. It can vary based on your property type and where it is located. Usually, the more remote your property, the more expensive the appraisal fee will be. The fee is usually about $500, but it can go as low as $350 and as high as $1,200 (or higher).

Hopefully this helps you understand the financial impact of obtaining a subprime mortgage. If you are going to go for it, make sure you run the numbers first to ensure it makes financial sense for you and your family.

Respectfully,
John and Jennifer

DEAR JOHN AND JENNIFER,

This is a lot of information and it looks like a lot of money. We'd like to explore a subprime second mortgage a bit more before we make any decisions. Where do we start and what steps do you recommend?

Sincerely,
Dick and Jane

DEAR DICK AND JANE,

Here is what we recommend:

1. Find out the interest rate, fees, term, and payment of the second mortgage. Be thorough. You will need to live with whatever is signed, so make you sure are comfortable with all the details.

2. Find out how much you would have to pay per month over the course of five years in order to pay off your second mortgage. Don't go any longer than that, if you can. You want to be out of debt as soon as possible.

3. Don't sign on the spot! Before you sign anything, examine all your other options. They include bank-

ruptcy, credit counselling, informal proposal, and consumer proposal. At this point you not only want to make sure that you make the best immediate decision for you and your family, but you also want to look at which long-term option is best for you to become debt-free.

4. Take some time, at least a week, to think over the options. You want to be comfortable with all the options in front of you so you can make the best possible decision.

In summary, obtaining a second subprime mortgage is an option, but you have to fully understand the costs and consequences. Take your time reading over the fine print.

We recommend that you seek out other solutions for your debts that may have a negative impact on your credit, but could be a better overall solution for you and your family.

Respectfully,
John and Jennifer

CHAPTER 6

This Is Going to HURT

DEAR JOHN AND JENNIFER,

Thanks for your advice. We sat down and reviewed all the details about getting a second mortgage. The more we look at it, the more uncomfortable we are with it.

We put all the numbers and fine print in front of us, and based on that, it just doesn't seem like the best option for us. As much as we don't want to damage our good credit rating, it looks like we may have no choice.

Can you tell us what our options are?

FYI: My credit score is 700 and Jane's is 724.

Sincerely,
Dick and Jane

DEAR DICK AND JANE,

We know this is a really difficult decision. If you're like most people, you've been told ever since you were little that having a good credit rating is critical to succeed in life. Admitting you may lose all those years of hard work can be difficult.

There are several things to keep in mind. First, remember that even though you have a high credit score right now, you're still unable to borrow, so having a good credit rating is of no more value to you than having a poor one. What you need is a way to get the necessary funds to get out of debt.

The options you have looked into (so far) are based on the bank's belief that you will be able to repay the money you are borrowing—and please don't get me wrong, you are following all the right steps by looking into these options first and discovering if they will work for you and your family.

But what if it is not possible for you to pay back any type of loan within a reasonable time period? What should you do then?

The next options will have a negative impact on your credit score.

In the following scenarios, you would no longer be receiving a "loan" but "financial restructuring" to manage your debt. Some people may tell you this won't affect your credit rating. That is simply not true; your credit score will be negatively impacted.

The next few options may be humbling because they force

you to admit you no longer have the ability to get yourself out of debt. So far, you've been paying your debts on time, and although it has been difficult, you have made at least your minimum monthly payments.

With each of the options below you may be advised to stop making payments on your unsecured debts. Before we go down that path, let's quickly review the difference between secured and unsecured debts.

Unsecured Debt:

- » Credit cards
- » Unsecured lines of credit
- » Overdraft
- » Income tax debts
- » Student loans
- » Payday loans
- » Personal loans

Secured Debt:

- » Mortgages
- » Secured lines of credit
- » Vehicle loans
- » Trailer loans

The best way to see if your debts are secured or unsecured is to review the original loan agreement. Sometimes if you have a mortgage and a credit card with the same bank, they may secure your credit card against your house. That means the credit card would be a secured item and cannot be included in the following options. Take the time to read those agreements before moving ahead.

Make sure you trust whoever is guiding you through this process. Ask for references and, if possible, make sure you're dealing with someone who is local. We have a lot of clients who came to us after they got bad advice from an out-of-province debt relief company.

In one situation, the company advised the client to stop paying their bills, which they did. The company then said to pay the money directly to them. A few months into this plan they received notice that their creditor was suing them.

The company they had hired to help them disappeared with their money!

Another common problem is that debt settlement companies will pressure debtors into believing "nonpayment" is the only option available. The debtor then stops paying their debts but soon realizes they were rushed into a bad decision. Had they taken more time to research other options, they could have received a consolidation loan from the bank.

But now that their debts haven't been paid for several months, their credit score has decreased, and no bank is willing to lend them the money. As we mentioned, do your due diligence and look at all the options before deciding which is best for you and your family.

Good luck and we look forward to hearing more from you soon.

Respectfully,
John and Jennifer

CHAPTER 7

Informal Proposals

DEAR JOHN AND JENNIFER,

Wow, dealing with this is way more complicated and serious than we thought. Can you please break down all these different options for us? We are worried about losing our credit score but we may have no other choice.

Sincerely,
Dick and Jane

DEAR DICK AND JANE,

Don't worry, you still have options. Another good one is to settle your debt for less than you owe. They call this an informal proposal. With an informal proposal, you or a third party comes to a settlement agreement directly with your creditors.

You may have heard horror stories about debt settlement companies who collect your money for months and then tell you they are out of business and can't help you.

How is this possible? Most Canadian and US debt settlement companies will tell clients to stop paying their current creditors and pay them instead. Once the debt settlement company collects 25% of the funds needed to settle your debt, they will finally approach your creditors and settle the debts one by one. There is absolutely no guarantee that the creditors will accept the informal settlement offer at 25%; they often want up to 80%.

The problem is, it can take years for a client to pay that amount of money. In your case, 25% of your debt would be $15,750. Given your current financial situation, can you imagine how long it would take to get that amount of money together?

If you get involved with any debt settlement company and then are told to stop paying your creditors, your creditors may take legal action to sue you, garnish your wages, or securitize your debt to an asset. And because this is an informal proposal, you have no court protection, so the debt settlement company will be unable to prevent you from being sued.

At that point, your only option would be to file for a bankruptcy or consumer proposal. What about the money you paid to the debt settlement company? Unfortunately, it's gone. More often than not, their fees and payments are non-refundable.

So is this option even worth considering? An informal proposal can be good if you have access to funds, but be careful. We have seen clients who hired a collection agency to settle the debt but never got the correct paperwork so, months later, they were contacted by a totally new collection agency requesting new funds.

In order to get a final settlement, you need a full and final settlement letter from the collection agency or directly from the creditor. Without it, you have no legal recourse and may need to pay those funds all over again. If you do not have a full and final settlement letter and confirmation the payment was received, there is a good chance that that payment will simply be applied to the debt and they will keep pursuing you for the remaining balance.

In summary, informal proposals can be good but they can also be a nightmare. If you have access to money to settle out 25%-80% of your debt (depending on who your creditors are), this could be a good option. But if you don't have access to such funds? We suggest you stay away for informal proposals and look for other solutions.

Respectfully,
John and Jennifer

CHAPTER 8

Credit Counseling

DEAR JOHN AND JENNIFER,

Yikes! Informal proposals sound kinda scary and are probably not the best option for us. There are so many companies claiming they can help us with our debts, but we're confused by all the different options!

How can we tell a good company from a bad one? What should we look for in a good debt management company?

Sincerely,

Dick and Jane

DEAR DICK AND JANE,

As part of the process, we should look at all of your options. I am sure you have seen the nonprofit credit counsellors' advertisements so it's important we review this option, as for some this option works, but as with anything it should first be compared to all the options available, and we have more to cover.

Nonprofit Credit Counselor / Orderly Payments of Debt

A nonprofit credit counsellor and orderly payments of debt (OPD) are both nonprofit organizations. Probably the biggest difference is that the OPD falls within the federal Bankruptcy and Insolvency Act (BIA), whereas credit counsellors do not.

If you are working with a credit counsellor, it's still possible for your creditors to opt in (or out) and decide at any point to pursue your debt through litigation, even though you may be paying on time and working through a payment plan.

With an OPD, however, because it goes through the courts, it is legally binding and your creditors are unable to change anything in that agreement.

Both programs will put you on a monthly payment plan to repay your debts in full over the course of four to five years. They also usually offer you a lower interest rate than you were receiving from your creditor. Being able to make the monthly payments is a must.

Both programs will work with you to create a budget. You

have to make enough income to afford the payment plan or you won't qualify.

When you have paid off all your debts through these programs, you will have a negative credit rating for three years after the debt has been paid off, per Equifax, which is one of three credit reporting agencies in Canada. OPD's impact on your credit rating is generally greater, however, it is part of the BIA and your debt plan is filed through the courts.

Both programs usually charge administration fees with interest, but they are generally much less than what you are currently paying to your creditors. With an OPD it's a flat 5% interest rate. Credit counsellors may be able to get a rate as low as zero, but it may be as high as 8%. On an average, however, it is around 4% to 5%. The good thing with both of these programs is there is a set time when you will become debt-free.

Fees

Both programs can include fees of around $50 per month, which is not enough to cover their operating costs, but they don't need your money for that purpose, as both of these organizations receive a significant amount of funding from your creditors.

The Osgoode Hall Law School had this to say in a 2011 research paper:

"In return for their work, the Credit Counselling Agencies (CCA) are paid by both the creditors and the debtors. From the creditors, they receive a percentage of whatever the debtors pay to the creditors, generally on the order of 20%. From the debtors, they ask for about 10% of the monthly payment made to the creditors."

So are these options worth investigating?

We would never recommend signing up with this program or any other without at least looking into bankruptcy and consumer proposals first. There are situations where these programs work, however, and I am glad we are covering it as an option.

Keep in mind, once you begin working with a third party to settle your debt, whether it's credit counselling, bankruptcy, or proposals, you won't be able to obtain a mortgage for some time or receive a loan (for, say, a vehicle) with a good interest rate.

By going to a third party you're sending a clear message to your creditors you can no longer meet your financial obligations. So it's important to consider the other alternatives outside the OPD and credit counselling options.

Respectfully,
John and Jennifer

CHAPTER 9

The "B" Word

DEAR JOHN AND JENNIFER,

Thanks for the added info about OPDs. We talked to them, but our payments would be over $1,500 per month over 48 months, which would have us paying back $72,000 and we only owe $63,000!

And of course, we still have our mortgage, car payments, food and our two children (plus another one on the way), so this is definitely not a good option for us. We were talking to some friends, and they said filing a bankruptcy is probably the easiest solution for us. All of our debts will just go away and we can walk away from it all.

That sounds too good to be true. Is it?

Sincerely,
Dick and Jane

DEAR DICK AND JANE,

We understand your frustration. You are right; your current debt repayment plan through the OPD does leave you with very little cash flow.

Before we talk about filing a bankruptcy, we should make sure you understand what it really means. It's a common perception that someone can simply go bankrupt and walk away from their debts. Unfortunately, it is more complicated than that.

When considering filing a bankruptcy, we need to look at how much your creditors would receive and how much you would pay per month. Most people don't know that while you are in bankruptcy you still have to pay your creditors something—and sometimes it can be quite a lot of money.

Financial Limitations While in Bankruptcy

While you're in bankruptcy, the federal government places limits on how much income you can keep each year. Each spring, the government releases income guidelines as to how much a person and/or a household under bankruptcy protection can make.

They will look at your net income, which is your after-tax income. **The 2017 guideline is as follows:**

NUMBER OF PERSONS IN THE HOUSE	ALLOWABLE NET INCOME PER MONTH
1	$2,121
2	$2,640
3	$3,246
4	$3,941
5	$4,470
6	$5041
7	$5,612

It's important to note that the government looks at the total household income and not just who is making more money. What happens if you make more than the allowed amount? You will have to pay the Licenced Insolvency Trustee 50% of that additional amount each month.

As you can see in our chart, as a family of four, you are allowed to make a net income of $3,941 per month. You mentioned in one of your earlier letters that you take home $5,000 per month. So here's how your bankruptcy payments would look.

$5,000 – MONTHLY COMBINED INCOME

- $3,941 – allowable monthly income

$1,059 – ineligible amount to take home

$1,059 × 50% = $529.50 – amount payable to Licenced Insolvency Trustee (LIT) each month

Given that your income is above the allowed amount and you have never been bankrupt before, you would be in a bankruptcy for 21 months. Assuming your income remained consistent, you would be obligated to pay $529.50 each month to the LIT for the duration of your bankruptcy.

If your family net monthly income were to decrease to the allowed amount of $3,941, then you would pay nothing extra, just the Licensed Insolvency Trustee Fees, and be in bankruptcy for as little as nine months.

Keep in mind that the government is operating under the assumption that you will not be bankrupt again, so if you declare bankruptcy again, you would be in bankruptcy for between 24 and 36 months.

If you receive any additional income (such as overtime, child tax benefits, a bonus at work, or a wage increase) during your bankruptcy that raises your monthly income, the trustee will collect 50% of any money earned above the allowed amount of $3,941.

In a bankruptcy the LIT will also be evaluating your assets to ensure you don't have assets over and above what is set out by the federal and provincial governments. These assets include:

1. Home Equity. Some provinces require that if your home is worth more than what is owed on your home, you are required to pay the difference to the trustee. For example, if your home is worth

$300,000 and your mortgage balance is $250,000, you could be required to pay $50,000 to the trustee for the benefit of your creditors, less an agreed percentage of hypothetical selling costs. However, in the case of a rental home, as it's considered an investment, any equity above the agreed hypothetical selling costs would have to be paid to the trustee for the benefit of the creditors.

2. Cash on hand could be required to be paid to the LIT if it is deemed a significant amount.

3. Paid off vehicles or equity in a vehicle could also have to be paid to your trustee. How much equity you would be able to have without it impacting your bankruptcy depends on what province you live in.

4. Mutual funds, stocks and investments would have to either be cashed out and paid to your trustee, or the cash out value would have to be paid to your trustee. So your company stock matching plan could be at risk. In some provinces the creditors don't have access to RESPs (registered education savings plans), but in others they do. In some provinces RRSPs (registered retirement savings plans) are protected from your creditors, but in others the past 12 months of contributions are not protected from your creditors. So in those provinces, if you have made any contributions to your RRSPs, you may be required to either

cash those funds out or pay that amount to your trustee.

5. Other assets that could affect how much you would have to pay towards your bankruptcy are: art, household furniture, farming equipment, business equipment (tools of the trade), time shares, quads, dirt bikes, trailers, boats, hot tubs, excess of clothing, jewellery, collectibles, insurance policies, foreign properties, investments, funds you have lent out.

Assets not only come into consideration when you file a bankruptcy, but also over the course of the bankruptcy until you are discharged. So if your home goes up in value while you are in bankruptcy, the Licenced Insolvency Trustee could sell your home, for the benefit of your creditors, up until you receive your discharge. Also, if you acquire an asset during your bankruptcy such as a gift, savings or any other asset listed above, it may have to be paid to the trustee for the benefit of your creditors in order for you to obtain your discharge.

There are two government-mandated counselling sessions that everyone who files a bankruptcy must attend. However, it's possible to do this in a larger setting; under the BIA, groups of up to 20 are allowed.

Tax Returns

When someone assigns themselves into bankruptcy they are required to file a tax return right away. If you receive a tax refund after filing, the trustee can have access to a portion of it. Once your bankruptcy is completed, you will be required to file a post-bankruptcy tax return. This is so you have a clean slate and can show there is nothing further owed to the Canadian Revenue Agency (CRA).

Monthly Income and Expense Reporting

It is your obligation to provide your bankruptcy trustee with a statement each month showing your income and expenses. You are also required to provide the trustee with supporting documentation of your income and certain expenses. Based on this information, your bankruptcy trustee will calculate your required monthly bankruptcy payment.

Self-Employed Complication

There are several specific rules that apply to self-employed debtors. You didn't say whether this is a sole proprietorship or a corporation, so we'll outline the rules for both.

1. If you are a non-discharged bankrupt, you cannot be a director of a corporation because of your ability to directly control expenses, salaries, and business assets. Why? You could potentially pay less into your bankruptcy while still receiving a large portion of your living expenses from the company. This would allow you to live the same lifestyle as before. If you are bankrupt, there would usually be some noticeable changes in how you are living. The government recognizes that directors control the direction of the

company, and a company cannot function without a director. Therefore, if you have your own corporation and you are considering filing a bankruptcy, you would either need to find someone to replace you as director or you would have to stop operating your company and open up a sole proprietorship. This usually isn't a problem unless your company needs to keep operating due to existing contracts or assets.

2. Under a bankruptcy, you cannot control your own business expenses. As a director, you may be the only one tracking your expenses, so it's possible to claim expenses for your business that benefit yourself (which may or may not be necessarily legitimate). If you have your own sole proprietorship, it is much harder. Let's say you are a realtor. Part of your business is to take clients out for meals. As a sole proprietor, you must submit your monthly income and expense form to a bankruptcy trustee at the end of every month. He or she can question all of your expenses and reserves the right to disallow certain transactions. Should that happen, those extra expenses would show up as added income, which means you would have to pay more into your bankruptcy.

3. Finally, as we mentioned, the more money you make, the more you need to pay toward your bankruptcy. This may make you less motivated to grow your busi-

ness or pick up new contracts, since half the money will go toward your bankruptcy.

Bankruptcy Is like a Bad Tattoo

Bankruptcies are very bad for your credit history. All of the debts you included in your bankruptcy will have the strongest negative credit rating possible placed beside them. Perhaps the bigger issue, however, is that the bankruptcy will remain on your credit bureau report for six years after it is finally discharged. If you declare bankruptcy for a second time, it will remain for 14 years.

This will affect your ability to borrow again in the future. There's a saying, "Once a bankrupt, always a bankrupt," because it tends to stick to you like a bad tattoo. For the rest of your life, you will have to disclose on a credit or employment application that you have filed for a bankruptcy. And if you ever file for a second bankruptcy, do not be surprised if the major mortgage lenders decline your application.

Do we ever recommend bankruptcies?

There are certain situations where we do. If someone is on a fixed income, for example, and there is little chance of their income increasing or decreasing. Also if someone simply has too much debt and the only payments they can afford are the bankruptcy payments, we would recommend it.

We recently had an elderly client whose only source of income was her pension of $957 per month. She was injured in a fall, which resulted in her being unable to return to work. Unfortunately, she did not qualify for disability benefits. Because she was unable to work and make her debt payments, she had an overdraft in her bank account of $500, which she was using up every month.

Thankfully her husband, who was debt-free, was able to help her by sharing the cost of their rent, bills, and some groceries. To make ends meet, she lived off her credit cards, and by the time she came into our office, she owed approximately $25,000, with an interest rate of 19.99%.

With monthly payments of $600, it would have taken her 72 months to pay off this debt. But she did not have an extra $600 a month to put toward debt payments. Even if she did pay, by the time she was finished, the total debt cost would be $42,840, of which the total interest paid would be $17,840.

It looked hopeless to her. Due to her age and her circumstances, with absolutely no plans or even the financial capability to borrow funds, she was a perfect candidate to file for a bankruptcy.

In summary, while bankruptcy may be the best option in some cases, it isn't the only option you have. It's important that you make an informed decision and consider all the factors at play, including payments, credit, monthly reporting, and the future consequences of being labeled as "a bankrupt" for life, even after it has been removed from your credit bureau and public records.

Sincerely,
John and Jennifer

CHAPTER 10

Consumer Proposals

DEAR JOHN AND JENNIFER,

We definitely didn't know how complex bankruptcies are. It sounds like it's not the best option for us. But we're getting desperate.

Are there any options left?

Sincerely,
Dick and Jane

DEAR DICK AND JANE,

Take heart. We have one more option for you to consider. It's called a consumer proposal, and it's the middle ground between a bankruptcy and an OPD.

The consumer proposal is an offer you make to your creditors to reduce the debt and offer a new repayment amount with new repayment terms that are affordable to you. It becomes a compromise between you and your creditors: you offer to pay back more than the creditors would receive in a bankruptcy and the creditors agree to reduce the debt and agree to new payment terms.

Generally it's a better option for your creditors because they recover more of the money you owe them. We know what you're asking: "Is it a good option for us?"

For example, in a bankruptcy, you would pay your creditors 20 cents on the dollar. In a consumer proposal, you could be paying them up to 35 cents on the dollar.

The amount being offered depends on a few factors: who your creditors are, how much you owe, how many members are in your family, and what other kinds of assets you own.

Your creditors have the right to make a counteroffer depending on the budget submitted and the cause of a person's insolvency.

How do they work?

They're open repayment plans where you pay no interest on your monthly payments over a span of up to five years. You can always pay it off early. The amount you pay back will not change. Unlike a bankruptcy, if your income increases or decreases, your payments will remain the same, with no penalties or interest.

Once your proposal is submitted through your licensed insolvency trustee, the creditors have 45 days to vote on your proposal if you owe under $250,000 without including your primary residence. However, if you owe over $250,000 then your creditors have 21 days to vote on your proposal. Since you owe less then $250,000, you just need 51% of your creditors to vote for the terms of your proposal and the other 49% of the creditors would be bound to the terms of the proposal.

Since you owe $63,684, it wouldn't be uncommon to have your debt reduced to approximately $36,000 over 60 months, which is $600 per month. However, I think you should try for a lower amount. As it is a negotiating process, with professional help and guidance you should be able to obtain an even lower proposal.

Another benefit of a proposal is that most of your payments towards your proposal, if not all of them, are made after you have a proposal accepted by your creditors.

Unlike a bankruptcy, you can also obtain credit while in a proposal as long as you inform your new creditor about your situation. If you're in a proposal that is in good standing, you can also support (and bring) family members to Canada.

If you're a licensed professional in a career where you simply cannot be bankrupt (e.g., financial advisor, CMA accountant, CA, psychologist), a consumer proposal is a great alternative.

Dick, the good news is that, because you're self-employed, you can stay on as the director of your corporation. Since you aren't filing for bankruptcy, you won't be required to fill out monthly expense sheets or tax returns at the start or end of the proposal. You are still required to be tax compliant as you would in any other situation. Make sure and faithfully file your taxes every year so you don't owe the CRA any future income tax debt or GST.

So what's the catch?

Your credit is still going to be negatively impacted, depending on the type of debt you owe. The consumer proposal will remain on your credit report for three years after it is paid off. The sooner you pay it off, the sooner the consumer proposal will get wiped off your credit report.

Q & A

We know you still have a lot of questions about consumer proposals, so here are some of the most common ones people ask us.

Could my creditors file a lawsuit against me?

A consumer proposal will protect you from being sued. Since it is filed through the courts under the Bankruptcy and

Insolvency Act, you're protected from your creditors as long as the proposal has been accepted (and approved) and you are maintaining your obligations.

What about my garnished wages?

Whatever has already been garnished is gone for good. The good news is, when a consumer proposal is filed, the garnishment will stop, even if you owe money to the government.

What are my obligations?

Never fall behind by more than three payments on your proposal or it's an automatic default. You will also have to attend two mandatory counselling sessions. They will include financial literacy topics such as creating a realistic and sustainable budgeting plan for your family, creating an emergency savings account, goal setting, and education on credit and how to rebuild and use it responsibly. Finally, if any income taxes are included in your proposal, you can never fall behind on your taxes or filings. You must also remain tax compliant and file your taxes every year.

Sounds like a pretty good deal, eh? If you ask our advice, after reviewing your case, we believe this is the best solution for you.

We suggest you take your time and review it against all the other options available.

Sincerely,
John and Jennifer

CHAPTER 11

Navigating Help

DEAR DICK AND JANE,

Thanks for sticking with us as we went over the best options for you. The majority of Canadians are in debt, so don't feel like you are stigmatized because you're in this situation. It's happened to practically all of us at one time or another.

So what's the next step?

A consumer proposal is a formal negotiation process between you and your creditors. It is a legal process governed by the Bankruptcy and Insolvency Act that must be filed by a Licensed Insolvency Trustee (formally Bankruptcy Trustee). It is legally binding and comes with protection against most garnishments and judgments. It also prevents creditors from attempting to collect on any of the debt, so those aggressive collection calls would stop. The dual role of the trustee is to investigate your financial situation and to ensure that your rights are not abused while also protecting the rights of your creditors. For consumers that have a strong understanding of the Bankruptcy and Insolvency Act and do not require comprehensive financial rehabilitation programs to reduce the impact on their credit rating, working directly with a trustee can be a good option. For those requiring their own independent advocate, additional support and compassion, and extended financial education/rehabilitation, working with an intermediary can be an excellent option.

We can guess your next question, and it's a great one and will help determine if you can do this alone or if you need additional support.

What is the difference between and Intermediary and a Licensed Insolvency Trustee?

So it's 100% clear, an intermediary cannot file a consumer proposal or bankruptcy. Only a Licensed Insolvency Trustee can do that. So why would you want an intermediary working for you?

Well, let us break it down for you.

A trustee is governed by the federal Bankruptcy and Insolvency Act (BIA). They have several statutory obligations under the Act. However, they cannot act as a financial advisor to someone like you struggling with consumer debt or help you get the best possible result when making a consumer proposal or a bankruptcy.

A good intermediary, on the other hand, uses many different trustees across Canada to file consumer proposals. The reason is that different trustees have different perspectives on the Bankruptcy and Insolvency Act. These perspectives can provide great flexibility with the proposals an intermediary can structure for a consumer like you, and may result in far greater savings for you as the consumer.

The other main difference is the after-care programs a good intermediary will offer. A good intermediary provides a comprehensive credit rebuilding and financial rehabilitation plan that will help ensure you're not left financially vulnerable in the future.

Because the trustee fees are tariffed, it is almost impossible for them to offer these types of after-care programs for the fees they receive.

It's easy to see that trustees' and intermediaries' services are complementary. A good intermediary will remove certain conflicts the trustee may face. Now the intermediary should solely represent the interest of the consumer, and then the consumer will receive the after-care they desperately need to create financial stability.

Hope that helps explain some of the details around this. As always, if you have any questions, please let us know.

Respectfully,
John and Jennifer

CHAPTER 12

Happy Rescue Stories

TESTIMONIAL #1

I was in debt for $116,000 after a bad marriage. My wife left me with a mortgage that I could not pay and I ended up in foreclosure. When I met with the trustee, they recommended that I go bankrupt but I didn't want to listen or to just give up. I'm glad that I hired John and Jennifer to help me instead. They represented me and helped reduce my CMHC mortgage shortfall debt down to $22,400. I didn't have to go bankrupt like the trustee recommended. My monthly payment is now $400 with NO interest! I am going be debt-free in less than 5 years!

Jason C.

TESTIMONIAL #2

Dear John and Jennifer,

Thank you for helping us with our debt. We were in such financial turmoil my wife and I could not sleep at night. We were depressed; our marriage was slowly falling apart. We had so much debt that sometimes we could not pay our utilities. They piled up to be two months in arrears. When I met you, you kindly explained your services to us, cut our debt and helped us rebuild our credit. You listened to us, never judged us, and explained that our relationship was completely confidential. You were sincere, professional and trustworthy. And above all else, you kept your word. Because of you, we are slowly putting our life back together and learning to live a comfortable life. Comfortable and cautious. We are still learning from our past mistakes and know that we now have a bright future ahead of us.

Thank you for helping us to see it.

Regards,
R & M Family

TESTIMONIAL #3

I was approximately $52,000.00 in debt. I was losing sleep at night worrying about all my bills. I was stressed a lot and sometimes I had trouble focusing at work. I chose to hire John and Jennifer to help me restructure my debt down to $8,400.

My one low monthly payment is now just $150 with 0% interest, and I have already started to rebuild my credit through their credit rebuilding program.

Dan H.

TESTIMONIAL # 4

Dear Jennifer,

Thank you so much for helping me with my debt! I was at the end of my rope when I met you. I was struggling with this financial difficulty for two years. I had three jobs and worked 16 hours a day; I was stressed all the time, and unable to focus; and I had marital conflict, just to name a few of my problems. You explained that I have options and can do something about this debt. Because of your help, I was able to reclaim my life. Literally, you have helped me live again. Thank you so much and God bless you.

Emily

TESTIMONIAL #5

Before I met Jennifer, my husband and I had $45,000 worth of debt. I was so helpless and depressed, I couldn't sleep well, I was feeling so stressed and my husband and I ended up fighting over how to pay our monthly bills. John and Jennifer helped us cut our debts, pay 0% interest and rebuild credit.

Right now, I'm back to my old self: less stressed, financially and emotionally satisfied, and with much better budgeting skills. We can now start saving for a better future for our kids. To Jen and John—a million thanks!

—S.Q. & M.Q.

TESTIMONIAL # 6

For the past year, my husband and I have tried to consolidate our debts. We were out of luck; the bank couldn't approve us. I was told by a friend to try a broker but we got the same response we'd gotten from the bank: "DECLINED." The broker gave us three pieces of advice: first, to find a credit counselor; second, to file bankruptcy; and last, sell the house. This was not what I wanted to do!

I did a search looking for options: I found three credit counselors but I wasn't really convinced their programs were the best option for me.

I didn't know what else to do. I did not want to lose hope. I wanted to believe there was still a chance for us to save our home, our marriage, our family and our reputation. Then I found John and Jennifer's advertisement. After I filled out a form, we were contacted by John and Jennifer the next day. My husband and I listened to their advice about my options and trusted them to handle our debt problems. We had no hesitation when we decided to hire them to represent us. They really looked out for our best interest.

We had an enormous debt that would take a long time to pay back. But because of their help, my debt was reduced from $35,400 to $8,400. My monthly payment is now down to $150. My husband's debt (that was originally $24,600) is now down to $7,840. His new monthly payment is now $140.00. We knew if we didn't get help from John and Jennifer, we would have to sacrifice a lot of years and a lot of extra money to pay off our debts. I'd rather be debt free sooner than later! With their budgeting help, we now maintain our monthly expenses and income according to our needs. Jennifer is also helping us rebuild our credit. You two are lifesavers. Thank you!

Sincerely,

D. Reyes

TESTIMONIAL #7

I used to dread hearing the ring of my telephone. It felt like there was always a bill collector wanting money. Before I met Jennifer, I had $43,000 worth of debt. I tried for years to make it go away. The stress was always there day and night. Whenever I would make any money, it would always get gobbled by the debt. When I met with John and Jennifer, I was able to see a way to have a real solution. They were able to explain things to me in a meaningful way without me feeling like I was being dehumanized. I have spoken to other so-called "experts" in the past who had very little clue how the financial world worked. John and Jennifer knew the options and helped me choose what was best for me. I have met with many other "experts" who have an agenda of selling their product, which was not the best product for me. For example, I have a friend who declared bankruptcy over $6,000! The "expert" she talked to wanted to sell a bankruptcy. She was bullied into doing it so the "expert" could get the sale, no matter how bad it was for my friend. John and Jennifer will never do that. They are people of integrity and I would trust their advice again in the future. If you want your freedom back—call John and Jennifer!

—*R.M.*

TESTIMONIAL #8

Before I called Jennifer I was up to my neck in debt. Not really understanding the true value of money and its worth made it very easy to rack up credit card debt. I got a second job and was struggling trying to pay over $700 monthly just making the minimum payments. After spending over a year stressed and tired from working 60 hours a week, I was referred to them by a friend. I explained my situation and they immediately took action! They took my debt from $32,000 to $9,600. My experience with Jennifer was amazing! She was very understandable and knowledgeable and was always available any time I had questions. Instead of paying over $700 per month towards my debt, I now pay $160. I've been able to quit my second job and actually start saving money. Doing a proposal with Jennifer's help was the smartest choice I've made.

V.F.

TESTIMONIAL #9

Over the last few years I had managed to run up $150,000.00 in unsecured debt. Mainly credit cards and lines of credit. I had approached the banks to secure a loan to pay off the debts, but because of the high minimum payments, I was not able to qualify for the payments, which would have been less than my minimum payments each month! Because of the high balances I was carrying, the interest rates kept creeping up and it was becoming a challenge just to make the minimum payments. I was losing sleep, and it was stressful for me and my family just trying to make ends meet. I was constantly searching the internet for solutions to my predicament when I came across John and Jennifer's website. I contacted them and they assured me over the phone that they could help me out. I must admit initially I was a little skeptical. I met with them and they were able to discuss various options. They seemed genuinely sympathetic to my situation. We were able to come up with a strategy whereby we would offer a proposal based on what I could afford to repay on a monthly basis over a 60-month period. The settlement was agreed to by all parties (a pleasant surprise as I was still somewhat skeptical) and now I have a fixed monthly payment schedule, repaying a portion of the total debt, interest-free. Having a strategy in place, and the ability to make my monthly payments has taken a huge burden off my back, and I sincerely thank John and Jennifer for all their help.

—PC

TESTIMONIAL #10

After my divorce, I found myself facing financial trouble—credit cards out of control, bill payments falling behind, not able to make ends meet. I was staring at over $60K in unpayable debt. Then I met John and Jennifer.

During our first meeting, they gave me options on how to fix my financial picture that consisted of debt repayment, debt reduction and a solid plan on how to rebuild my credit future. With their help, I am now on the road to financial recovery and looking forward to my clean slate. Without John and Jennifer's help, I'm not sure where I'd be today.

Sincerely,
Cie

TESTIMONIAL #11

Every day I am so thankful that I met you. My husband and I were in way over our heads, drowning in a sea of debt, and it was only getting worse. We didn't know what to do anymore. I was even afraid to answer the phone. How could we let it get this bad? We couldn't sleep anymore and it was starting to affect our jobs, our relationships with our family and friends, and especially our marriage. We tried everything to get out of debt, including using all our retirement savings, but nothing was working. All it did was make us feel worse. We still had the debt and now we had no retirement fund. Finally, we caught a break when we met you. Right from the start, you made us feel like you were there to help. You were amazing to talk to and didn't make us feel bad for our situation. You always treated us in a caring, professional manner, offering solutions, not criticism. You explained all our options and helped us choose the best solution for us and our situation, and the best part was that no matter how many questions we asked, you were always there to answer and guide us.

Because of you both I am now able to enjoy life again and my marriage is stronger than ever. I can even answer my phone again without fear of who is on the other end. My husband and I sleep so much better and have even been able to start thinking about our retirement again. You did exactly what you said you would do and for that we will always be grateful. I highly recommend your services to anyone who wants an honest, professional opinion and someone who truly cares working on this difficult situation.

Thanks again for everything.

Regards,
KN

TESTIMONIAL #12

From the very first phone call, I could tell immediately that John and Jennifer were highly professional, yet warm, engaging and genuinely interested in their clients' needs. Through my experience with them I have been consistently impressed with their level of service and how specifically they tailored their scope of work to my particular needs.

Before I met John and Jennifer I had interviewed two other financial consultants, and in comparison with them the others could not hold a candle, and I mean that very definitely. One of the service providers was clearly not client-focused, and the other one lacked knowledge. John and Jennifer met all of my needs including being client-focused and highly knowledgeable.

On top of that, both John and Jennifer and their office manager Lily are genuinely pleasant people, and their personalities are well suited to the kind of business they are in, assisting people with debt management. This can be a stressful time for their clients, yet through it all they give their clients a sense of calm assuredness, which ensured I felt that I was being supported by people who truly cared.

I highly recommend them!

K.G.

CONNECT WITH US!

Find us on Facebook:

f John Jennifer Croft

Website:

www.fromdebttolife.com

Made in the USA
Columbia, SC
31 July 2017